HISTORY'S MOST INFLUENTIAL WOMEN

FROM Ancient Egypt TO 1500

Hatshepsut to Isabella I

EDITED BY KATHLEEN KUIPER

Britannica® Educational Publishing

IN ASSOCIATION WITH

ROSEN EDUCATIONAL SERVICES

Published in 2024 by Britannica Educational Publishing
(a trademark of Encyclopædia Britannica, Inc.)
in association with Rosen Educational Services, LLC
2544 Clinton Street, Buffalo, NY 14224

Distributed exclusively by Rosen Educational Services.
For a listing of additional Britannica Educational Publishing titles, call toll free (800) 237-9932.

First Edition

Britannica Educational Publishing
Michael I. Levy: Executive Editor
Marilyn L. Barton: Senior Coordinator, Production Control
Steven Bosco: Director, Editorial Technologies
Lisa S. Braucher: Senior Producer and Data Editor
Yvette Charboneau: Senior Copy Editor
Kathy Nakamura: Manager, Media Acquisition
Kathleen Kuiper: Manager, Arts and Culture

Editor: Kathleen Kuiper
Book design: Michael Flynn

Photo credits: Cover https://en.wikipedia.org/wiki/File:Nofretete_Neues_Museum.jpg.

Cataloging-in-Publication Data

Names: Kuiper, Kathleen.
Title: From Ancient Egypt to 1500—Hatshepsut to Isabella I / edited by Kathleen Kuiper.
Description: New York : Britannica Educational Publishing, in Association with Rosen Educational Services. 2024. | Series: History's most influential women | Includes glossary and index.
Identifiers: ISBN 9781641900669 (library bound) | ISBN 9781641900652 (pbk) | ISBN 9781641900676 (ebook)
Subjects: LCSH: Women--Biography--Juvenile literature. | Women--Biography--To 500--Juvenile literature. | Women--History--Middle Ages, 500-1500--Juvenile literature. | Women--History--Juvenile literature.
Classification: LCC HQ1123.K87 2024 | DDC 920.72 B--dc23

Manufactured in the United States of America

CPSIA Compliance Information: Batch #CWBRIT24. For further information contact Rosen Publishing at 1-800-237-9932.

CONTENTS

Introduction

"Reserve your right to think, for even to think wrongly is better than not to think at all."—Hypatia (370–415)

The world is filled with fascinating women, and each woman has her own compelling story. This book, filled with profiles of striking individuals who serve as outstanding representatives of their gender, covers many of the most outstanding, influential women from around the globe who lived between the 15th century BCE and 1500 CE. Coverage runs from queens to commoners.

Most of these women managed to flourish in the face of adversity. For centuries, merely being a woman was an obstacle to power. Consider the case of Hatshepsut, the eldest daughter of the ancient Egyptian King Thutmose I and his queen, Ahmose. After her father and half brother died, Hatshepsut was allowed to assume the role of regent only because the rightful heir, her son, was an infant. She took full advantage of the situation, essentially claiming the throne for herself while nominally coruling with her son. For a woman, Hatshepsut wielded unprecedented power. Court artists took to depicting her as a man, full beard and all.

Another ruler of Egypt, Cleopatra, rose to power when she was 18 years old, coruling with her brother, Ptolemy XIII. As the eldest sibling by eight years, Cleopatra quickly became the dominant ruler, much to Ptolemy XIII's displeasure. It did not take long for Ptolemy to forcibly remove Cleopatra from her position. The young queen did not take this coup lying down. She fled to Syria, where she promptly gathered an army and returned to confront her brother in a successful attempt to reclaim the throne.

Restored to power after forcing Ptolemy to flee Alexandria, Cleopatra fortified her position through clever political and romantic alliances with future emperor Julius Caesar and the Roman general Mark Antony. Although forced to share power with first her brothers, then her son, Cleopatra proved to be the true driving force behind the Egyptian throne for 22 years.

Other women became influential rulers directly through marriage or by giving birth. Eleanor of Aquitaine, for example, had considerable power as the wife and mother of several reigning kings of France and England. As the daughter of William X, the duke of Aquitaine, Eleanor inherited a large portion of western France upon his death. In 1137, she married the heir to the throne of France, Louis VII, and became queen of France. When the marriage was annulled in 1152, she married the heir to the throne of England, Henry II, and became queen of England. She and Louis had two daughters, but she and Henry produced three daughters and five sons, including Richard the Lion-Heart, and John, both of whom would become kings of England. Her daughters also married into the royal families of Bavaria, Castile, and Sicily.

The influence of these women, and the others profiled in this book, reverberates throughout the ages. Their leadership has served to enrich, enlighten, and shape modern society. These amazing and influential individuals have given all of us, men and women alike, something to admire and strive for in our own lives.

HATSHEPSUT

(fl. 15th century BCE)

The most famous female king of Egypt was Hatshepsut (Hatchepsut), who reigned in her own right *circa* 1473–1458 BCE. She attained unprecedented power for a woman, adopting the full titles and regalia of a pharaoh.

Hatshepsut was the elder daughter of the 18th-dynasty king Thutmose I and his consort Ahmose, and she was married to her half brother Thutmose II, son of the lady Mutnofret. Since three of Mutnofret's older sons had died prematurely, Thutmose II inherited his father's throne about 1492 BCE, with Hatshepsut as his consort. Hatshepsut bore one daughter, Neferure, but no son. When her husband died about 1479 BCE, the throne passed to his son Thutmose III, born to Isis, a lesser harem queen. As Thutmose III was an infant, Hatshepsut acted as regent for the young king.

For the first few years of her stepson's reign, Hatshepsut was an entirely conventional regent. But by the end of his seventh regnal year, she had assumed the kingship and adopted a full royal titulary (the royal protocol adopted by Egyptian sovereigns). Hatshepsut and Thutmose III were now corulers of Egypt, with Hatshepsut very much the dominant king. Hitherto Hatshepsut had been depicted as a typical queen, with a female body and appropriately feminine garments. But now, after a brief period of experimentation that involved combining a female body with kingly (male) regalia, her formal portraits began to show Hatshepsut with a male body, wearing the traditional regalia of kilt, crown or head-cloth, and false beard. To dismiss this as a serious attempt to pass herself off as a man is to misunderstand Egyptian artistic convention, which showed things not as they were but as they should be. In causing herself to be depicted as a traditional king,

Hatshepsut ensured that this is what she would become.

In styling herself as a king, Hatshepsut avoided the epithet "mighty bull," regularly employed by other kings. Although in her reliefs she was depicted as a male, pronominal references in the texts usually reflect her womanhood. Similarly, much of her statuary shows her in male form, but there are rarer examples that render her as a woman. In less formal documents she was referred to as "King's Great Wife"—that is, "Queen"—while Thutmose III was "King." There is thus a certain ambiguity in the treatment of Hatshepsut as king.

Hatshepsut never explained why she took the throne or how she persuaded Egypt's elite to accept her new position. However, an essential element of her success was a group of loyal officials, many handpicked, who controlled all the key positions in her government. Most prominent amongst these was Senenmut, overseer of all royal works and tutor to Neferure.

Traditionally, Egyptian kings defended their land against the enemies who lurked at Egypt's borders. Hatshepsut's reign was essentially a peaceful one, and her foreign policy was based on trade rather than war. But scenes on the walls of her Dayr al-Baḥrī temple, in western Thebes, suggest that she began with a short, successful military campaign in Nubia. More complete scenes show Hatshepsut's seaborne trading expedition to Punt, a trading center (since vanished) on the East African coast beyond the southernmost end of the Red Sea. Gold, ebony, animal skins, baboons, processed myrrh, and living myrrh trees were brought back to Egypt, and the trees were planted in the gardens of Dayr al-Baḥrī.

Restoration and building were important royal duties. Hatshepsut claimed, falsely, to have restored the damage wrought by the Hyksos (Asian) kings during their rule in Egypt. She undertook an extensive building program. In

Thebes this focused on the temples of her divine father, the national god Amon-Re. At the Karnak temple complex, she remodeled her earthly father's hypostyle hall, added a barque shrine (the Red Chapel), and introduced two pairs of obelisks. At Beni Hasan in Middle Egypt, she built a rock-cut temple known in Greek as Speos Artemidos. Her supreme achievement was her Dayr al-Baḥrī temple; designed as a funerary monument for Hatshepsut, it was dedicated to Amon-Re and included a series of chapels dedicated to the gods Osiris, Re, Hathor, and Anubis and to the royal ancestors. Hatshepsut was to be interred in the Valley of the Kings, where she extended her father's tomb so that she could be buried with him.

Toward the end of her reign, Hatshepsut allowed Thutmose to play an increasingly prominent role in state affairs; following her death, Thutmose III ruled Egypt alone for 33 years. At the end of his reign, an attempt was made to remove all traces of Hatshepsut's rule. Her statues were torn down, her monuments were defaced, and her name was removed from the official king list. Early scholars interpreted this as an act of vengeance, but it seems that Thutmose was ensuring that the succession would run from Thutmose I through Thutmose II to Thutmose III without female interruption. Hatshepsut sank into obscurity until 1822, when the decoding of hieroglyphic script allowed archaeologists to read the Dayr al-Baḥrī inscriptions. Initially the discrepancy between the female name and the male image caused confusion, but today the Thutmoside succession is well understood.

NEFERTITI

(fl. 14th century BCE)

Nefertiti, also called Neferneferuaten-Nefertiti. was the queen of Egypt and wife of King Akhenaton (formerly Amenhotep IV; reigned *circa* 1353–1336 BCE), and she played a prominent role in the cult of the sun god (Aton, or Aten) that he established.

Nefertiti's parentage is unrecorded, but, as her name translates as "A Beautiful Woman Has Come," early Egyptologists believed that she must have been a princess from Mitanni (Syria). There is strong circumstantial evidence, however, to suggest that she was the Egyptian-born daughter of the courtier Ay, brother of Akhenaton's mother, Tiy. In any case, it is known that she had a younger sister, Mutnodjmet. Married to him before her husband's accession, Nefertiti bore six daughters within 10 years of her marriage, the elder three being born at Thebes, the younger three at Tell el-Amarna. Two of her daughters became queens of Egypt.

The earliest images of Nefertiti come from the Theban tombs of the royal butler Parennefer and the vizier Ramose, where she is shown accompanying her husband. In the Theban temple known as Hwt-Benben ("Mansion of the Benben Stone"; the benben was a cult object associated with solar ritual), Nefertiti played a more prominent role, usurping kingly privileges in order to serve as a priest and offer to the Aton, represented by the sun's disk. A group of blocks recovered from Karnak (Luxor) and Hermopolis Magna (Al-Ashmunayn) shows Nefertiti participating in the ritual smiting of the female enemies of Egypt. She wears her own unique headdress— a tall, straight-edged, flat-topped blue crown.

By the end of Akhenaton's fifth regnal year, the Aton had become Egypt's dominant national god. The old state temples were closed and the court transferred to a purpose-built capital city, Akhetaton (Amarna). Here Nefertiti continued to play an important religious role, worshipping alongside her husband and serving as the female element in the divine triad formed by the god Aton, the king Akhenaton, and his queen. Her sexuality, emphasized by her exaggeratedly feminine body shape and her fine linen garments, and her fertility, emphasized by the constant appearance of the six princesses, indicate that she was considered a living fertility goddess. Nefertiti and the royal family appeared on private devotional stelae and on the walls of nonroyal tombs, and images of Nefertiti stood at the four corners of her husband's sarcophagus.

Some historians, having considered her reliefs and statuary, believe that Nefertiti may have acted as queen regnant—her husband's coruler rather than his consort. However, the evidence is by no means conclusive, and there is no written evidence to confirm her political status.

Soon after Akhenaton's 12th regnal year, one of the princesses died, three disappeared (and are also presumed to have died), and Nefertiti vanished. The simplest inference is that Nefertiti also died, but there is no record of her death and no evidence that she was ever buried in the Amarna royal tomb. Early Egyptologists, misunderstanding the textual evidence recovered from the Maru-Aten sun temple at Amarna, deduced that Nefertiti had separated from Akhenaton and had retired to live either in the north palace at Amarna or in Thebes. This theory is now discredited. Others have suggested that she outlived her husband, took the name Smenkhkare, and ruled alone as female king before handing the throne to Tutankhamen. There is good evidence for a King Smenkhkare, but the identification in the 20th century of a male body buried in the Valley of the Kings as Tutankhamen's brother makes it unlikely that Nefertiti and Smenkhkare were the same person.

Nefertiti's body has never been discovered. Had she died at Amarna, it seems inconceivable that she would not have been buried in the Amarna royal tomb. But the burial in the Valley of the Kings confirms that at least one of the Amarna burials was reinterred at Thebes during Tutankhamen's reign. Egyptologists have therefore speculated that Nefertiti may be one of the unidentified bodies recovered from the caches of royal mummies in the Valley of the Kings. In the early 21st century, attention focused on the "Younger Lady" found in the tomb of Amenhotep II, although it is now accepted that this body is almost certainly too young to be Nefertiti.

Amarna was abandoned soon after Akhenaton's death, and Nefertiti was forgotten until, in 1912, a German archaeological mission led by Ludwig Borchardt discovered a portrait bust of Nefertiti lying in the ruins of the Amarna workshop of the sculptor Thutmose. The bust went on display at the Egyptian Museum in Berlin in the 1920s and immediately attracted worldwide attention, causing Nefertiti to become one of the most recognizable and, despite a missing left eye, most beautiful female figures from the ancient world.

SAPPHO

(b. *ca.* 610 BCE, Lesbos [Greece]—d. *ca.* 570 BCE)

The Greek lyric poet Sappho (or Psappho, as her name is given in the Aeolic dialect spoken by the poet) has been greatly admired in all ages for the beauty of her writing style. She ranks with Archilochus and Alcaeus, among Greek poets, for her ability to impress readers with a lively sense of her personality. Her language contains elements from Aeolic vernacular speech and Aeolic poetic tradition, with traces of epic vocabulary familiar to readers of Homer. Her phrasing is concise, direct, and picturesque. She has the ability to stand aloof and judge critically her own ecstasies and grief, and her emotions lose nothing of their force by being recollected in tranquillity.

Legends about Sappho abound, many having been repeated for centuries. She is said, for example, to have been married to Cercylas, a wealthy man from the island of Andros. But many scholars challenge this claim, finding evidence in the Greek words of the bawdry of later comic poets. Most modern critics also consider it legend that Sappho leaped from the Leucadian rock to certain death in the sea because of her unrequited love of Phaon, a younger man and a sailor. She had at least two brothers, Larichus and Charaxus, and may have had a third. A fragment from Sappho that is dedicated to Charaxus has survived. One of her poems mentions a daughter named Cleis or Claïs. The tradition that she fled the island or was banished and went to Sicily may be true, but she lived most of her life in her hometown of Mytilene on Lesbos.

Sappho's work contains only a few apparent allusions to the political disturbances of the time, which are so frequently reflected in the verse of her contemporary Alcaeus. Her themes are invariably personal—primarily concerned with her *thiasos*, the usual term (not found in Sappho's extant writings) for the female community, with a religious and educational background, that met under her leadership. Sappho herself attacks in her poems other *thiasoi* directed by other women.

The goal of the Sapphic *thiasos* is the education of young women, especially for marriage. Aphrodite is the group's tutelary divinity and inspiration. Sappho is the intimate and servant of the goddess and her intermediary with the girls. In the ode to Aphrodite, the poet invokes the goddess to appear, as she has in the past, and to be her ally in persuading a girl she desires to love her. Frequent images in Sappho's poetry include flowers, bright garlands, naturalistic outdoor scenes, altars smoking with incense, perfumed unguents to sprinkle on the body and bathe the hair—that is, all the elements of Aphrodite's rituals. In the *thiasos* the girls were educated and initiated into grace and elegance for seduction and love. Singing, dancing, and poetry played a central role in this educational process and other cultural occasions. As was true for other female communities, including the Spartan, and for the corresponding masculine institutions, the practice of homoeroticism within the *thiasos* played a role in the context of initiation and education.

In Sappho's poetry, love is passion, an inescapable power that moves at the will of the goddess. It is desire and sensual emotion, nostalgia and memory of affections that are now distant but shared by the community of the *thiasos*. There is a personal poetic dimension, which is also collective because all the girls of the group recognize themselves in it. An important part of Sappho's poetic oeuvre is occupied by epithalamia, or nuptial songs.

It is not known how her poems were published and circulated in her own lifetime and for the following three or four centuries. In the era of Alexandrian scholarship (3rd and 2nd centuries BCE), what survived of her work was collected and published in a standard edition of nine books of lyrical verse, divided according to meter. This edition did not endure beyond the early Middle Ages. By the 8th or 9th century CE, Sappho was represented only by quotations in other authors. Only the ode to Aphrodite, which is 28 lines long, is complete. The next longest fragment is 16 lines long. Since 1898 these fragments have been greatly increased by papyrus finds, though, in the opinion of some scholars, nothing equal in quality to the two longer poems.

CLEOPATRA

(b. 70/69 BCE—d. August of 30 BCE, Alexandria, Egypt)

Noted in history and drama as the lover of Julius Caesar and later the wife of Mark Antony, Cleopatra became queen on the death of her father, Ptolemy XII Auletes, in 51 BCE. She ruled successively with her two brothers, Ptolemy XIII (51–47) and Ptolemy XIV (47–44), and her son Ptolemy XV Caesar (44–30). Cleopatra actively influenced Roman politics at a crucial period, and she came to represent, as did no other woman of antiquity, the prototype of the romantic femme fatale.

Early Life and Reign

The Greek name Cleopatra means "Famous in Her Father," and her full regnal name is Cleopatra VII Thea Philopator ("Cleopatra the Father-Loving Goddess"). She was destined to become the last queen of the Macedonian dynasty that ruled Egypt between the death of Alexander the Great in 323 BCE and its annexation by Rome in 30 BCE. The line had been founded by Alexander's general Ptolemy, who became King Ptolemy I Soter of Egypt. Cleopatra was of Macedonian descent and had little, if any, Egyptian blood, although the Classical author Plutarch wrote that she alone of her house took the trouble to learn Egyptian and, for political reasons, styled herself as the new Isis, a title that distinguished her from the earlier Ptolemaic queen Cleopatra III, who had also claimed to be the living embodiment of the goddess Isis. Coin portraits of Cleopatra show a countenance alive rather than beautiful, with a sensitive mouth, firm chin, liquid eyes, broad forehead, and prominent nose.

When Ptolemy XII died in 51 BCE, the throne passed to his young son, Ptolemy XIII, and daughter, Cleopatra

VII. It is likely, but not proven, that the two married soon after their father's death, a practice common among royalty. The 18-year-old Cleopatra, older than her brother by about eight years, became the dominant ruler. Evidence shows that the first decree in which Ptolemy's name precedes Cleopatra's was in October 50 BCE. Soon after, Cleopatra was forced to flee Egypt for Syria, where she raised an army and in 48 BCE returned to face her brother at Pelusium, on Egypt's eastern border. The murder of the Roman general Pompey, who had sought refuge from Ptolemy XIII at Pelusium, and the arrival of Julius Caesar brought temporary peace.

A Powerful Alliance

Cleopatra realized that she needed Roman support, or, more specifically, Caesar's support, if she was to regain her throne. Each was determined to use the other. Caesar sought money for repayment of the debts incurred by Cleopatra's father, Auletes, as he struggled to retain his throne. Cleopatra was determined to keep her throne and, if possible, to restore the glories of the first Ptolemies and recover as much as possible of their dominions, which had included southern Syria and Palestine.

Caesar and Cleopatra became lovers and spent the winter besieged in Alexandria. Roman reinforcements arrived the following spring, and Ptolemy XIII fled and drowned in the Nile. Cleopatra, now married to her brother Ptolemy XIV, was restored to her throne. In June 47 BCE she gave birth to Ptolemy Caesar (known to the people of Alexandria as Caesarion, or "little Caesar"). Whether Caesar was the father of Caesarion, as his name implies, cannot now be known.

It took Caesar two years to extinguish the last flames of Pompeian opposition. As soon as he returned to Rome, in

46 BCE, he celebrated a four-day triumph—the ceremonial in honor of a general after his victory over a foreign enemy—in which Arsinoe, Cleopatra's younger and hostile sister, was paraded. Cleopatra paid at least one state visit to Rome, accompanied by her husband-brother and son. She was accommodated in Caesar's private villa beyond the Tiber River and may have been present to witness the dedication of a golden statue of herself in the temple of Venus Genetrix, the ancestress of the Julian family to which Caesar belonged. Cleopatra was in Rome when Caesar was murdered in 44 BCE.

Antony and Cleopatra

Soon after her return to Alexandria, in 44 BCE, Cleopatra's coruler, Ptolemy XIV, died. Cleopatra now ruled with her infant son, Ptolemy XV Caesar. When, at the Battle of Philippi in 42 BCE, Caesar's assassins were routed, Mark Antony became the heir apparent of Caesar's authority—or so it seemed, for Caesar's great-nephew and personal heir, Octavian, was but a sickly boy. Antony, now controller of Rome's eastern territories, sent for Cleopatra so that she might explain her role in the aftermath of Caesar's assassination. She set out for Tarsus in Asia Minor loaded with gifts, having delayed her departure to heighten Antony's expectation. She entered the city by sailing up the Cydnus River in a barge while dressed in the robes of the new Isis. Antony, who equated himself with the god Dionysus, was captivated. Forgetting his wife, Fulvia, who in Italy was doing her best to maintain her husband's interests against the growing menace of young Octavian, Antony returned to Alexandria, where he treated Cleopatra not as a "protected" sovereign but as an independent monarch.

In Alexandria, Cleopatra and Antony formed a society

of "inimitable livers" whose members lived what some historians have interpreted as a life of debauchery and folly and others have interpreted as lives dedicated to the cult of the mystical god Dionysus.

In 40 BCE Cleopatra gave birth to twins, whom she named Alexander Helios and Cleopatra Selene. Antony had already left Alexandria to return to Italy, where he was forced to conclude a temporary settlement with Octavian. As part of this settlement, he married Octavian's sister, Octavia (Fulvia having died). Three years later, Antony was convinced that he and Octavian could never come to terms. His marriage to Octavia now an irrelevance, he returned to the east and reunited with Cleopatra. Antony needed Cleopatra's financial support for his postponed Parthian campaign. In return, Cleopatra requested the return of much of Egypt's eastern empire, including large portions of Syria and Lebanon and even the rich balsam groves of Jericho.

The Parthian campaign was a costly failure, as was the temporary conquest of Armenia. Nevertheless, in 34 BCE Antony celebrated a triumphal return to Alexandria. This was followed by a celebration known as "the Donations of Alexandria." Crowds flocked to the Gymnasium to see Cleopatra and Antony seated on golden thrones on a silver platform with their children sitting on slightly lower thrones beside them. Antony proclaimed Caesarion to be Caesar's son—thus relegating Octavian, who had been adopted by Caesar as his son and heir, to legal bastardy. Cleopatra was hailed as queen of kings, Caesarion as king of kings. Alexander Helios was awarded Armenia and the territory beyond the Euphrates, his infant brother Ptolemy the lands to the west of it. The boys' sister, Cleopatra Selene, was to be ruler of Cyrene. It was clear to Octavian, watching from Rome, that Antony intended his extended family to rule the civilized world. A propaganda war erupted. Octavian seized Antony's will (or what he claimed to be Antony's will) from the temple of the Vestal Virgins, to whom it had been entrusted, and revealed to the Roman people that not only had Antony bestowed Roman possessions on a foreign woman but intended to be buried beside her in Egypt. The rumor quickly spread that Antony also intended to transfer the capital from Rome to Alexandria.

Antony and Cleopatra spent the winter of 32–31 BCE in Greece. The Roman Senate deprived Antony of his prospective consulate for the following year, and it then declared war against Cleopatra. The Battle of Actium, in which Octavian faced the combined forces of Antony and Cleopatra on September 2, 31 BCE, was a disaster for the Egyptians. Antony and Cleopatra fled to Egypt, and Cleopatra retired to her mausoleum as Antony went off to fight his last battle. Receiving the false news that Cleopatra had died, Antony fell on his sword. In a last excess of devotion, he had himself carried to Cleopatra's retreat and there died, after bidding her to make her peace with Octavian.

Cleopatra buried Antony and then committed suicide. The means of her death is uncertain, though Classical writers came to believe that she had killed herself by means of an asp, symbol of divine royalty. She was 39 and had been a queen for 22 years and Antony's partner for 11. They were buried together, as both of them had wished, and with them was buried the Roman Republic.

Cleopatra Through the Ages

The vast majority of Egypt's many hundreds of queens, although famed throughout their own land, were more or less unknown in the outside world. As the dynastic age ended and the hieroglyphic script was lost, the queens' stories were forgotten and their monuments buried under

Egypt's sands. But Cleopatra had lived in a highly literate age, and her actions had influenced the formation of the Roman Empire; her story could not be forgotten. Octavian (the future emperor Augustus) was determined that Roman history should be recorded in a way that confirmed his right to rule. To achieve this, he published his own autobiography and censored Rome's official records. As Cleopatra had played a key role in his struggle to power, her story was preserved as an integral part of his, but it was diminished to just two episodes: her relationships with Julius Caesar and Mark Antony. Cleopatra, stripped of any political validity, was to be remembered as an immoral foreign woman who tempted upright Roman men. As such, she became a useful enemy for Octavian, who preferred to be remembered for fighting against foreigners rather than against his fellow Romans.

This official Roman version of a predatory, immoral Cleopatra passed into Western culture, where it was retold and reinterpreted as the years passed, until it evolved into a story of a wicked life made good by an honorable death. Meanwhile, Muslim scholars, writing after the Arab conquest of Egypt about 640 CE, developed their own version of the queen. Their Cleopatra was first and foremost a scholar and a scientist, a gifted philosopher and a chemist.

Plutarch's *Parallel Lives*, translated from the Greek into French by Jacques Amyot (1559) and then from the French into English by Sir Thomas North (1579), served as the inspiration behind Shakespeare's play *Antony and Cleopatra* (1606–07). Shakespeare dropped some of Plutarch's disapproval and allowed his queen to become a true heroine. His was by no means the first revision of Cleopatra, nor was it to be the last, but his is the Cleopatra that has lingered longest in the public imagination. From Shakespeare stems a wealth of Cleopatra-themed art—plays, poetry, paintings, and operas.

In the 20th century, Cleopatra's story was preserved and further developed through film. Many actresses, including Theda Bara (1917), Claudette Colbert (1934), and Elizabeth Taylor (1963), have played the queen, typically in expensive, exotic films that concentrate on the queen's love life rather than her politics. Meanwhile, Cleopatra's seductive beauty—a seductive beauty that is not supported by the queen's contemporary portraiture—has been used to sell a wide range of products, from cosmetics to cigarettes. In the late 20th century, Cleopatra's racial heritage became a subject of intense academic debate, with some African American scholars embracing Cleopatra as a Black African heroine.

MARY

(fl. beginning of the Christian, or Common, Era)

The Virgin Mary and Saint Mary are among the many names by which Mary, the mother of Jesus, is known. She has been an object of veneration in the Christian church since the apostolic age and a favorite subject in Western art, music, and literature. Mary is known from biblical references, which are, however, too sparse to construct a coherent biography. The development of the doctrine of Mary can be traced through titles that have been ascribed to her in the history of the Christian communions—guarantee of the incarnation, virgin mother, second Eve, mother of God, ever virgin, immaculate, and assumed into heaven.

The New Testament account of her humility and obedience to the message of God have made her an exemplar for all ages of Christians. Out of the details supplied in the New Testament by the Gospels about the maid of Galilee, Christian piety and theology have constructed a picture of Mary that fulfills the prediction ascribed to her in the Magnificat (Luke 1:48): "Henceforth all generations will call me blessed."

The first mention of Mary is the story of the Annunciation, which reports that she was living in Nazareth and was betrothed to Joseph (Luke 1:26 ff.); the last mention of her (Acts 1:14) includes her in the company of those who devoted themselves to prayer after the ascension of Jesus into heaven. Other stories about her recount her visit with Elizabeth, her kinswoman and the mother of John the Baptist, the precursor of Jesus (Luke 1:39 ff.); the birth of Jesus and the presentation of him in the Temple (Luke 2:1 ff.); the coming of the Magi and the flight to Egypt (Matthew 2:1 ff.); the Passover visit to Jerusalem when Jesus was 12 years old (Luke 2:41 ff.); the marriage at Cana in Galilee, although her name is not used (John 2:1 ff.); the attempt to see Jesus while he was teaching (Mark 3:31 ff.); and the station at the cross, where, apparently widowed, she was entrusted to the disciple John (John 19:26 ff.). Even if one takes these scenes as literal historical accounts, they do not add up to an integrated portrait of Mary. Only in the narratives of the Nativity and the Passion of Christ is her place a significant one. In contrast, her acceptance of the privilege conferred on her in the Annunciation is the solemn prologue to the Christmas story. Not only does she stand at the foot of the Cross, but in the Easter story, "the other Mary" who came to the tomb of Jesus (Matthew 28:1) is not she; according to traditional interpretations, she knew that the body of Jesus would not be there. On the other hand, the incidents that belong to the life of Jesus contain elements of a pronouncedly human character, perhaps even the suggestion that she did not fully understand Jesus' true mission.

Since the early days of Christianity, however, the themes that these scenes symbolize have been the basis for thought and contemplation about Mary. Christian communions and theologians differ from one another in their interpretations of Mary principally on the basis of where they set the terminal point for such development and expansion—that is, where they maintain that the legitimate development of doctrine may be said to have ended.

Mary has achieved great cultural importance. Popular devotion to Mary—in such forms as feasts, devotional services, and the rosary—has played a tremendously important role in the lives of Roman Catholics and the Orthodox; at times, this devotion has pushed other doctrines into the background. Modern Roman Catholicism has emphasized that the doctrine of Mary is not an isolated belief but must be seen in the context of two other Christian doctrines: the doctrine of Christ and the doctrine of the church. What is said of Mary is derived from what is said of Jesus: this was the basic meaning of Theotokos. She has also been known as "the first believer" and as the one in whom the humanity of the church was representatively embodied.

HYPATIA

(b. *ca.* 370, Alexandria, Egypt—d. March 415, Alexandria)

The Egyptian Neoplatonist philosopher Hypatia was also the first notable woman in the field of mathematics.

The daughter of Theon, also a notable mathematician and philosopher, Hypatia became the recognized head of the Neoplatonist school of philosophy at Alexandria about 400, and her eloquence, modesty, and beauty, combined with her remarkable intellectual gifts, attracted a large number of pupils. Among them was Synesius of Cyrene, afterward bishop of Ptolemais (*circa* 410), several of whose letters to her are still extant.

Hypatia lectured on mathematics and on the

philosophical teachings of two Neoplatonists: Plotinus (*circa* 205–270 CE), the founder of Neoplatonism, and Iamblichus (*circa* 250–330 CE), the founder of the Syrian branch of Neoplatonism. She symbolized learning and science, which at that time in Western history were largely identified with paganism.

This left Hypatia in a precarious situation. Theodosius I, Roman emperor in the East from 379 to 392 and then emperor in both the East and West until 395, initiated an official policy of intolerance to paganism and Arianism in 380. In 391, in reply to Theophilus, the bishop of Alexandria, he gave permission to destroy Egyptian religious institutions. Christian mobs obliged by destroying the Library of Alexandria, the Temple of Serapis, and other pagan monuments. Although legislation in 393 sought to curb violence, particularly the looting and destruction of Jewish synagogues, a renewal of disturbances occurred after the accession of Cyril to the patriarchate of Alexandria in 412. Tension culminated in the forced, albeit illegal, expulsion of Alexandrian Jews in 414 and the murder of Hypatia, the most prominent Alexandrian pagan, by a fanatical mob of Christians in 415. The departure soon afterward of many scholars marked the beginning of the decline of Alexandria as a major center of ancient learning.

According to the *Suda Lexicon*, a 10th-century encyclopedia, Hypatia wrote commentaries on the *Arithmetica* of Diophantus of Alexandria, on the *Conics* of Apollonius of Perga, and on an astronomical canon (presumably Ptolemy's *Almagest*). We have it on the authority of her father, Theon, that she revised Book III of his commentary on the *Almagest*. All of these works are lost, although some may survive as parts of the extant Arabic versions of the *Arithmetica*. The known titles of her works, combined with the letters of Synesius who consulted her about the construction of an astrolabe and a hydroscope (identified in the 17th century by Pierre de Fermat as a hydrometer), indicate that she devoted herself particularly to astronomy and mathematics. The existence of any strictly philosophical works by her is unknown. Indeed, her philosophy was more scholarly and scientific in its interest and less mystical and intransigently pagan than the Neoplatonism taught in other schools. Nevertheless, statements attributed to her, such as "Reserve your right to think, for even to think wrongly is better than not to think at all" and "To teach superstitions as truth is a most terrible thing," must have incensed Cyril, who in turn incensed the mob.

Hypatia's reputation as a learned and beautiful female philosopher, combined with the dramatic details of her grisly death, have inspired the imaginations of numerous writers, inspiring works such as Charles Kingsley's novel *Hypatia: New Foes with an Old Face* (1852).

THEODORA

(b. *ca.* 497 — d. June 28, 548, Constantinople [now Istanbul, Turkey])

The Byzantine empress Theodora was the wife of the emperor Justinian I (reigned 527–565) and probably the most powerful woman in Byzantine history. Her intelligence and political acumen made her Justinian's most trusted adviser and enabled her to use the power and influence of her office to promote religious and social policies that favored her interests.

Little is known of Theodora's early life, but a combination of the official version with that found in the highly colored *Secret History* of Procopius of Caesarea probably provides the best explanation. Her father was a bear keeper at the Hippodrome (circus) in Constantinople. She became an actress while still young, leading an unconventional life that included giving birth to at least one child out of wedlock. For a time, she made her living as a wool spinner. When Justinian met her, she had been converted to monophysitism, a nonorthodox doctrine. Attracted by her beauty and intelligence, he made her his mistress, raised her to the rank of patrician, and in 525 married her. When Justinian succeeded to the throne in 527, she was proclaimed Augusta.

Theodora exercised considerable influence, and though she was never coregent, her superior intelligence and deft handling of political affairs caused many to think that it was she, rather than Justinian, who ruled Byzantium. Her name is mentioned in nearly all the laws passed during that period. She received foreign envoys and corresponded with foreign rulers, functions usually reserved for the emperor. Her influence in political affairs was decisive, as illustrated in the Nika revolt of January 532. The two political factions in Constantinople, the Blues and the Greens, united in their opposition to the government and set up a rival emperor. Justinian's advisers urged him to flee, but Theodora advised him to stay and save his empire, whereupon Justinian's general, Belisarius, herded the rioters into the Hippodrome and cut them to pieces.

Theodora is remembered as one of the first rulers to recognize the rights of women, passing strict laws to prohibit the traffic in young girls and altering the divorce laws to give greater benefits to women. She spent much of her reign trying to mitigate the laws against the monophysites. Though she succeeded in ending their persecution in 533, she never succeeded in changing Justinian's religious policy from its emphasis on orthodoxy and friendship with Rome.

The best-known representation of Theodora is the mosaic portrait in the Church of San Vitale in Ravenna. Her death, possibly from cancer or gangrene, was a severe blow to Justinian. Her importance in Byzantine political life is shown by the fact that little significant legislation dates from the period between her death and that of Justinian (565).

WUHOU

(b. 624, Wenshui [now in Shanxi province], China—d. Dec. 16, 705, Luoyang)

Wuhou is the posthumous name (*shi*) of the woman who rose from concubinage to become empress of China during the Tang dynasty (618–907). She ruled effectively for many years, the last 15 (690–705) in her own name. During her reign, Tang rule was consolidated, and the empire was unified.

Wu Zhao, also called Wu Zetian, entered the palace of the Tang emperor Taizong (ruled 626–649) in 638, at age 14, as a junior concubine. By that time, the Tang dynasty had recently reunited China, largely through the efforts of Taizong. Little is known of Wu's life as a concubine of Taizong, but, on his death in 649, she is traditionally said to have already entered into intimate relations with his heir, the Gaozong emperor. Relegated to a Buddhist convent on the death of Taizong, as custom required, the future empress Wuhou was visited there by the new emperor, who had her brought back to the palace to be his own favorite concubine. She first eliminated her female rivals within the palace—the existing empress and leading concubines—and in 655 gained the position of empress for herself, eventually bearing Gaozong four sons and one daughter.

Wuhou used her authority to bring about the fall of the elder statesmen, all of whom had served Taizong and still exercised great influence over the government. These men opposed her elevation to the position of empress, mainly because, although she was the daughter of a relatively senior officer, her family was not one of the great aristocratic clans. They also objected to the nature of her relationship with Gaozong, on the grounds that as she had been a concubine of Taizong, it was incestuous. By 660 the empress had triumphed over all opponents, who had been dismissed, exiled, and, in many instances, finally executed. Even the emperor's uncle, the head of the great family of the Changsun, of imperial descent, was hounded to death, and his relatives were exiled or ruined.

Virtually supreme power was now exercised by the Wuhou empress in the name of the sickly Gaozong, who was often too ill to attend to state affairs for long periods. The emperor, who was weak in character, relied on her entirely, and for the last 23 years of his life, the empress was the real ruler of China. She continued to eliminate potential rivals, even when these were her own relatives, but she governed the empire with great efficiency, employing able men who clearly felt loyalty to her and stood by her when she was challenged. Her great ability as an administrator, her courage, decisive character, and readiness to use ruthless means against any opponent, however highly placed, won her the respect, if not the love, of the court.

In the years between 655 and 675, the Tang empire conquered Korea under military leaders who were picked and promoted by the empress. When Gaozong died in 683, he was succeeded by his son Li Xian (by Wuhou), known as the Zhongzong emperor. The new emperor had been married to a woman of the Wei family, who now sought to put herself in the same position of authority as that of Wuhou, for Zhongzong was as weak and incompetent as his father. After one month, Wuhou deposed her son, exiled him, and installed as emperor her second son, Li Dan (the Ruizong emperor), whose authority was purely nominal. A revolt was raised by Tang loyalists and ambitious young officials in the south. It was crushed within weeks with the loyal cooperation of the main armies of the throne. This demonstration of the support she commanded in the public service made the position of the empress unshakable.

Six years later, in 690, at age 65, the empress usurped the throne itself. Accepted without revolt, she ruled for 15 years. During that period the question of the succession began to assume great urgency. Her own nephews of the Wu family had hoped that as she had already changed the name of the dynasty to Zhou, she would also displace the Tang heirs of the Li family and leave the throne to one of the Wu nephews. Neither of them nor their sons was popular or unusually capable; on the other hand, Wuhou's own sons, the two former emperors Zhongzong and Ruizong, had little support and less ability. But, even among her loyal supporters, there was a growing hope that the Tang family of Li would not be discarded. In 698 the empress decided to accede to these views; the exiled Zhongzong was recalled to court and made crown prince. The empress showed her remarkable quality in this decision; she did not place her own family in the line of succession or designate one of her nephews as her heir. She seems to have had no ambition on behalf of her own family, only a determination to retain power for herself to the end.

In the last years of her life, from 699, the empress gave her favor to the Zhang brothers, artistic but depraved courtiers who engaged her affection by elaborate entertainments and skillful flattery. They were intensely resented by the court and senior officials, many of whom had the temerity—and courage—to warn the empress of their pernicious activity. She did not heed these warnings and, as she gradually fell into ill health, depended increasingly on the care of the Zhang brothers. In February 705, a conspiracy formed among the leading ministers and generals, who seized the palace, executed the Zhang brothers, and compelled the empress, old and ill, to yield power to Zhongzong, who reigned until 710. She retired to another palace and died there in December of that year.

The Wuhou empress was a highly competent ruler, using men of her own choice, regardless of their social standing. Although her motives were to secure her own authority, the consequences of her policies were to be of great historical importance. The transformation of Chinese society in the Tang period from one dominated by a military and political aristocracy to one governed by a scholarly bureaucracy drawn from the gentry was promoted by her policy. The significance of this aspect of her rule was long obscured by the prejudice of Chinese historians against an usurping empress and her many acts of cruelty toward opponents. She established the new unified empire on a lasting basis and brought about needed social changes that stabilized the dynasty and ushered in one of the most fruitful ages of Chinese civilization.

IRENE

(b. *ca.* 752, Athens [Greece]—d. Aug. 9, 803, Lesbos)

Irene was a Byzantine ruler and saint of the Greek Orthodox Church who was instrumental in restoring the use of icons in the Eastern Roman Empire.

The wife of the Byzantine emperor Leo IV, Irene became, on her husband's death in September 780, guardian of their 10-year-old son, Constantine VI, and co-emperor with him. Later in that year she crushed what seems to have been a plot by the Iconoclasts (opposers of the use of icons) to put Leo's half brother, Nicephorus, on the throne.

Irene favored the restoration of the use of icons, which had been prohibited in 730. She had Tarasius, one of her supporters, elected patriarch of Constantinople and then summoned a general church council on the subject. When it met in Constantinople in 786, it was broken up by Iconoclast soldiers stationed in that city. Another council, which is recognized by both the Roman Catholic and Eastern Orthodox churches as the Seventh Ecumenical Council, met at Nicaea in 787 and restored the cult of images.

As Constantine approached maturity, he grew resentful of his mother's controlling influence in the empire. An attempt to seize power was crushed by the empress, who demanded that the military oath of fidelity should recognize her as senior ruler. Anger at the demand prompted the themes (administrative divisions) of Asia Minor to open resistance in 790. Constantine VI was proclaimed sole ruler and his mother banished from court. In January 792, however, Irene was allowed to return to court and even to resume her position as coruler. By skillful intrigues with the bishops and courtiers she organized a conspiracy against Constantine, who was arrested and blinded at his mother's orders (797).

Irene then reigned alone as emperor (not empress) for five years. In 798 she opened diplomatic relations with the Western emperor Charlemagne, and in 802 a marriage between her and Charlemagne was reportedly contemplated. According to the contemporary Byzantine historian Theophanes, the scheme was frustrated by one of Irene's favorites. In 802 a conspiracy of officials and generals deposed her and placed on the throne Nicephorus, the minister of finance. She was exiled, first to the island of Prinkipo (now Büyükada) and then to Lesbos.

Irene's zeal in restoring icons and her patronage of monasteries ensured her a place among the saints of the Greek Orthodox Church. Her feast day is August 9.

MURASAKI SHIKIBU

(b. *ca.* 978, Kyōto, Japan—d. *ca.* 1014, Kyōto)

The court lady known as Murasaki Shikibu was the author of the *Genji monogatari* (*The Tale of Genji*), generally considered the greatest work of Japanese literature and thought to be the world's oldest full novel.

The author's real name is unknown; it is conjectured that she acquired the sobriquet of Murasaki from the name of the heroine of her novel, and the name Shikibu reflects her father's position at the Bureau of Rites. She was born into a lesser branch of the noble and highly influential Fujiwara family and was well educated, having learned Chinese (generally the exclusive sphere of males). She married a much older distant cousin, Fujiwara Nobutaka, and bore him a daughter, but after two years of marriage he died.

Some critics believe that she wrote the entire *Tale of Genji* between 1001 (the year her husband died) and 1005, the year in which she was summoned to serve at court (for reasons unknown). It is more likely that the composition of her extremely long and complex novel extended over a much greater period; her new position within what was then a leading literary center likely enabled her to produce a story that was not finished until about 1010. In any case this work is the main source of knowledge about her life. It possesses considerable interest for the delightful glimpses it affords of life at the court of the empress Jōtō mon'in, whom Murasaki Shikibu served.

The Tale of Genji captures the image of a unique society of ultrarefined and elegant aristocrats, whose indispensable accomplishments were skill in poetry, music, calligraphy, and courtship. Much of it is concerned with the loves of Prince Genji and the different women in his life, all of whom are exquisitely delineated. Although the novel does not contain scenes of powerful action, it is permeated with a sensitivity to human emotions and to the beauties of nature hardly paralleled elsewhere. The tone of the novel darkens as it progresses, indicating perhaps a deepening of Murasaki Shikibu's Buddhist conviction of the vanity of the world. Some, however, believe that its last 14 chapters were written by another author.

Arthur Waley was the first to translate *The Tale of Genji* into English (6 vol., 1925–33). Waley's translation is beautiful and inspiring, a classic of English literature, but also very free. Edward Seidensticker's translation (1976) is true to the original in both content and tone, but its notes and reader aids are sparse, unlike the translation published by Royall Tyler in 2001. Murasaki Shikibu's diary is included in *Diaries of Court Ladies of Old Japan* (1935), translated by Annie Shepley Ōmori and Kōchi Doi.

HILDEGARD

(b. 1098, Böckelheim, West Franconia [Germany]—d. Sept. 17, 1179, Rupertsberg, near Bingen; traditional feast day September 17)

Hildegard, also called Hildegard von Bingen and the Sibyl of the Rhine, was a German abbess, visionary mystic, and composer. Born of noble parents, Hildegard was educated at the Benedictine cloister of Disibodenberg by Jutta, an anchorite and sister of the count of Spanheim. Hildegard was 15 years old when she began wearing the Benedictine habit and pursuing a religious life. She succeeded Jutta as prioress in 1136.

Having experienced visions since she was a child, at age 43 she consulted her confessor, who in turn reported the matter to the archbishop of Mainz. A committee of theologians subsequently confirmed the authenticity of Hildegard's visions, and a monk was appointed to help her record them in writing. The finished work, *Scivias*

(1141–1152), consists of 26 visions that are prophetic and apocalyptic in form and in their treatment of such topics as the church, the relationship between God and man, and redemption. About 1147, Hildegard left Disibodenberg with several nuns to found a new convent at Rupertsberg, where she continued to exercise the gift of prophecy and to record her visions in writing.

A talented poet and composer, Hildegard collected 77 of her lyric poems, each with a musical setting composed by her, in *Symphonia armonie celestium revelationum*. Her numerous other writings include lives of saints; two treatises on medicine and natural history, reflecting a quality of scientific observation rare at that period; and extensive correspondence, in which are to be found further prophecies and allegorical treatises. She also for amusement contrived her own language. She traveled widely throughout Germany, evangelizing to large groups of people about her visions and religious insights. Though her earliest biographer proclaimed her a saint and miracles were reported during her life and at her tomb, she was never formally canonized. She is, however, listed as a saint in the Roman Martyrology and is honored on her feast day in certain German dioceses.

As one of the few prominent women in medieval church history, Hildegard became the subject of increasing interest in the latter half of the 20th century. Her writings were widely translated into English; several recordings of her music were made available; and works of fiction, including Barbara Lachman's *The Journal of Hildegard of Bingen* (1993) and Joan Ohanneson's *Scarlet Music: A Life of Hildegard of Bingen* (1997), were published.

ELEANOR OF AQUITAINE

(b. *ca.* 1122—d. April 1, 1204, Fontevrault, Anjou, France)

The queen consort of both Louis VII of France (1137–52) and Henry II of England (1152–1204), Eleanor of Aquitaine (also called Eleanor of Guyenne) was the mother of Richard the Lion-Heart and John of England. She was perhaps the most powerful woman in 12th-century Europe.

Eleanor (French: Éléonore, or Aliénor, d'Aquitaine [or de Guyenne]) was the daughter and heiress of William X, duke of Aquitaine and count of Poitiers, who possessed one of the largest domains in France—larger, in fact, than those held by the French king. Upon William's death in 1137, she inherited the duchy of Aquitaine and in July 1137 married the heir to the French throne, who succeeded his father, Louis VI, the following month. Eleanor became queen of France, a title she held for the next 15 years. Beautiful, capricious, and adored by Louis, Eleanor exerted considerable influence over him, often goading him into undertaking perilous ventures.

From 1147 to 1149, Eleanor accompanied Louis on the Second Crusade to protect the fragile Latin kingdom of Jerusalem, founded after the First Crusade only 50 years before, from Turkish assault. Eleanor's conduct during this expedition, especially at the court of her uncle Raymond of Poitiers at Antioch, aroused Louis's jealousy and marked the beginning of their estrangement. After their return to France and a short-lived reconciliation, their marriage was annulled in March 1152. According to feudal customs, Eleanor then regained possession of Aquitaine, and two months later she married the grandson of Henry I of England, Henry Plantagenet, count of Anjou and duke of Normandy. In 1154 he became, as Henry II, king of England, with the result that England, Normandy, and the west of France were united under his rule.

Eleanor had only two daughters by Louis VII; to her new husband she bore five sons and three daughters. The sons were William, who died at the age of three; Henry; Richard, the Lion-Heart; Geoffrey, duke of Brittany; and John, surnamed Lackland until, having outlived all his brothers, he inherited, in 1199, the crown of England. The daughters were Matilda, who married Henry the Lion, duke of Saxony and Bavaria; Eleanor, who married Alfonso VIII, king of Castile; and Joan, who married successively William II, king of Sicily, and Raymond VI, count of Toulouse. Eleanor would well have deserved to be named the "grandmother of Europe."

During her childbearing years, she participated actively in the administration of the realm and even more actively in the management of her own domains. She was instrumental in turning the court of Poitiers, then frequented by the most famous troubadours of the time, into a center of poetry and a model of courtly life and manners. She was the great patron of the two dominant poetic movements of the time: the courtly love tradition, conveyed in the romantic songs of the troubadours, and the historical *matière de Bretagne*, or "legends of Brittany," which originated in Celtic traditions and in the *Historia regum Britanniae*, written by the chronicler Geoffrey of Monmouth sometime between 1135 and 1138.

The revolt of her sons against her husband in 1173 put her cultural activities to a brutal end. Since Eleanor, 11 years her husband's senior, had long resented his infidelities, the revolt may have been instigated by her; in any case, she gave her sons considerable military support. The revolt failed, and Eleanor was captured while seeking refuge in the kingdom of her first husband, Louis VII. Her semi-imprisonment in England ended only with the death of Henry II in 1189. On her release, Eleanor played a greater political role than ever before. She actively prepared for Richard's coronation as king, was administrator of the realm during his Crusade to the Holy Land, and, after his capture by the duke of Austria on Richard's return from the East, collected his ransom and went in person to escort him to England. During Richard's absence, she succeeded in keeping his kingdom intact and in thwarting the intrigues of his brother John Lackland and Philip II Augustus, king of France, against him.

In 1199 Richard died without leaving an heir to the throne, and John was crowned king. Eleanor, nearly 80 years old, fearing the disintegration of the Plantagenet domain, crossed the Pyrenees in 1200 in order to fetch her granddaughter Blanche from the court of Castile and marry her to the son of the French king. By this marriage she hoped to ensure peace between the Plantagenets of England and the Capetian kings of France. In the same year, she helped to defend Anjou and Aquitaine against her grandson Arthur of Brittany, thus securing John's French possessions. In 1202 John was again in her debt for holding Mirebeau against Arthur, until John, coming to her relief, was able to take him prisoner. John's only victories on the Continent, therefore, were due to Eleanor. She died in 1204 at the monastery at Fontevrault, Anjou, where she had retired after the campaign at Mirebeau.

Her contribution to England extended beyond her own lifetime. After the loss of Normandy (1204), it was her own ancestral lands and not the old Norman territories that remained loyal to England. She has been misjudged by many French historians who have noted only her youthful frivolity, ignoring the tenacity, political wisdom, and energy that characterized the years of her maturity. "She was beautiful and just, imposing and modest, humble and elegant"; and, as the nuns of Fontevrault wrote in their necrology, a queen "who surpassed almost all the queens of the world."

MARGARET I

(b. 1353, Søborg, Den.—d. Oct. 28, 1412, Flensburg)

As the regent of Denmark (from 1375), of Norway (from 1380), and of Sweden (from 1389), Margaret I, by diplomacy and war, pursued dynastic policies that led to the Kalmar Union (1397), which united Denmark, Norway, and Sweden until 1523 and Denmark and Norway until 1814.

The daughter of King Valdemar IV of Denmark, Margaret was only six years old when she was betrothed to Haakon, king of Norway and son of King Magnus Eriksson of Sweden and Norway. The betrothal, intended to counter the dynastic claims to the Scandinavian thrones by the dukes of Mecklenburg and the intrigues of certain aristocratic factions within the Scandinavian countries, was imperilled by the renewal in 1360 of the old struggle between Valdemar of Denmark and Magnus of Sweden. But military reverses and the opposition of his own nobility forced Magnus to suspend hostilities in 1363. The wedding of Margaret and Haakon took place in Copenhagen in the same year.

Haakon's aspirations to become king of Sweden were thwarted when he and his father were defeated soon afterward by Albert of Mecklenburg, who bore the Swedish crown from 1364 to 1389. Haakon, however, succeeded in keeping his Norwegian kingdom, and it was there that Margaret spent her youth, under the tutelage of Märta Ulfsdotter, a daughter of the Swedish saint, Bridget. Margaret early displayed her talent as a ruler: she soon overshadowed her husband and appears to have exercised the real power. The couple's only child, Olaf, was born in 1370.

After her father's death in 1375, Margaret—over the objections of the Mecklenburgian claimants—was successful in getting Olaf elected to the Danish throne. Following Haakon's death in 1380, Margaret also ruled Norway in her son's name. Thus began the Danish-Norwegian union that lasted until 1814. Margaret secured and extended her sovereignty: in 1385 she won back the economically important strongholds on the west coast of Scandia from the Hanseatic League, and for a time she was also able to safeguard Denmark's southern borders by agreement with the counts of Holstein.

Margaret and Olaf, who came of age in 1385, were on the point of making war on Albert to enforce their claims to the Swedish throne when Olaf died unexpectedly in 1387. Deploying all her diplomatic skill, Margaret consolidated her position, becoming regent of both Norway and Denmark and, in the absence of an heir, adopting her six-year-old nephew, Erik of Pomerania. She then joined forces with the Swedish nobles, who had risen against the unpopular king Albert in a dispute over the will disposing of the lands of Bo Jonsson Grip, the powerful chancellor. By the Treaty of Dalaborg of 1388, the nobles proclaimed Margaret Sweden's "sovereign lady and rightful ruler" and granted her the main portion of Bo Jonsson Grip's vast domains.

Defeating Albert in 1389, Margaret took him captive and released him only after the conclusion of peace six years later. His supporters, who had allied themselves with pirate bands in the Baltic Sea, did not surrender Stockholm until 1398.

Margaret was now the undisputed ruler of the three Scandinavian states. Her heir, Erik of Pomerania, was proclaimed hereditary king of Norway in 1389 and was elected king of Denmark and Sweden (which also included Finland) in 1396. His coronation took place the following year in the southern Swedish town of Kalmar, in the presence of the leading figures of all the Scandinavian countries.

At Kalmar the nobility manifested its opposition to Margaret's increasing exercise of absolute power. The two extant documents disclose traces of the struggle between two political principles: the principle of absolute hereditary monarchy, as expressed in the so-called coronation act, and the constitutional elective kingship preferred by some nobles, as expressed in the so-called union act. The Kalmar assembly was a victory for Margaret and absolutism; the union act—perhaps the medieval Scandinavian document most debated by historians—denoted a plan that failed.

Despite Erik's coronation, Margaret remained Scandinavia's actual ruler until her death. Her aim was to further develop a strong royal central power and to foster the growth of a united Scandinavian state with its center of gravity located in Denmark, her old hereditary dominion. She succeeded in eliminating the opposition of the nobility, in curbing the powers of the council of state, and in consolidating the administration through a network of royal sheriffs. In order to secure her position economically, she levied heavy taxes and confiscated church estates and lands exempt from dues to the crown. That such a policy succeeded without fatal strife to the union testifies to her strong political position as well as to her diplomatic skills and her ruthlessness. By adroitly using her relations to the Holy See, she was able to strengthen her influence over the church and on the politically important episcopal elections.

Margaret's political acumen was also evident in foreign affairs. Her main goals were to put an end to German expansion to the north and to extend and secure Denmark's southern borders, goals she tried to achieve through diplomatic means. An armed conflict did, however, break out with Holstein, and during the war Margaret died unexpectedly in 1412.

One of Scandinavia's most eminent monarchs, Margaret was able not only to establish peace in her realms but also to maintain her authority against the aspirations of German princes and against the superior economic power of the Hanseatic League. The united kingdom that she created and left as a legacy, whose cementing factor was a strong monarchy, remained in existence until 1523, albeit not without interruptions.

CHRISTINE DE PISAN

(b. 1364, Venice [Italy]—d. *ca.* 1430)

One of the earliest feminists, Christine de Pisan was a prolific and versatile French poet and author whose diverse writings include numerous poems of courtly love, a biography of Charles V of France, and several works championing women.

Christine's Italian father was astrologer to Charles V, and she spent a pleasant, studious childhood at the French court. At 15 she married Estienne de Castel, who became court secretary. Widowed after 10 years of marriage, she took up writing in order to support herself and her three young children. Her first poems were ballades of lost love written to the memory of her husband. These verses met with success, and she continued writing ballads, rondeaux, lays, and complaints in which she expressed her feelings with grace and sincerity. Among her patrons were Louis I, the duke d'Orléans, the duke de Berry, Philip II the Bold of Burgundy, Queen Isabella of Bavaria, and, in England, the 4th earl of Salisbury. In all, she wrote 10 volumes in verse, including *L'Épistre au Dieu d'amours* (1399; Letter to the God of loves), in which she defended women against the satire of Jean de Meun in the *Roman de la rose*.

Christine's prose works include *Le Livre de la cité des*

dames (1405; *The Book of the City of Ladies*), in which she wrote of women known for their heroism and virtue, and *Le Livre des trois vertus* (1405; Book of three virtues), a sequel comprising a classification of women's roles in medieval society and a collection of moral instructions for women in the various social spheres. The story of her life, *L'Avision de Christine* (1405), told in an allegorical manner, was a reply to her detractors. At the request of the regent, Philip the Bold of Burgundy, Christine wrote the life of the deceased king, Charles—*Le Livre des fais et bonnes meurs du sage roy Charles V* (1404; Book of the deeds and good morals of the wise King Charles V), a firsthand picture of Charles V and his court. Her eight additional prose works reveal her remarkable breadth of knowledge.

After the disastrous Battle of Agincourt in 1415, she retired to a convent. Her last work, *Le Ditié de Jehanne d'Arc* (written in 1429), is a lyrical, joyous outburst inspired by the early victories of Joan of Arc; it is the only such French-language work written during Joan's lifetime.

JOAN OF ARC

(b. *ca.* 1412, Domrémy, Bar, France—d. May 30, 1431, Rouen; canonized May 16, 1920; feast day May 30; French national holiday, second Sunday in May)

Joan of Arc (French: Jeanne d'Arc) is a national heroine of France, perhaps more significant for her contribution to the history of human courage than to the political and military history of France. She was a peasant girl who, believing that she was acting under divine guidance, led the French army in a momentous victory at Orléans that repulsed an English attempt to conquer France during the Hundred Years' War. Captured a year afterward, Joan was burned by the English and their French collaborators as a heretic. She became the greatest national heroine of her compatriots. Her achievement was a decisive factor in the later awakening of French national consciousness.

Joan was the daughter of a tenant farmer. In her mission of expelling the English and their Burgundian allies from the Valois kingdom of France, she felt herself to be guided by the "voices" of Saint Michael, Saint Catherine, and Saint Margaret. She possessed many attributes characteristic of the female visionaries who were a noted feature of her time. These qualities included extreme personal piety, a claim to direct communication with the saints, and a consequent reliance upon individual experience of God's presence beyond the ministrations of the priesthood and the confines of the institutional church. But to these were added remarkable mental and physical courage, as well as a robust common sense. Known as La Pucelle, or the Maid, of Orléans, Joan became in the following centuries a focus of unity for the French people, especially at times of crisis.

Joan's Mission

The crown of France at the time was in dispute between the dauphin Charles (later Charles VII), son and heir of the Valois king Charles VI, and the Lancastrian English king Henry VI. Henry's armies were in alliance with those of Philip the Good, duke of Burgundy (whose father, John the Fearless, had been assassinated in 1419 by partisans of the Dauphin), and were occupying much of the northern part of the kingdom. The apparent hopelessness of the Dauphin's cause at the end of 1427 was increased by the fact that, five years after his father's death, he had not been crowned. Reims, the traditional place for the investiture of French kings, was well within the territory held by his enemies. As long as the Dauphin remained unconsecrated, his claim to be king of France was open to challenge.

Joan's village of Domrémy was on the frontier between the France of the Anglo-Burgundians and that of the Dauphin. The villagers had already had to abandon their homes before Burgundian threats. Led by her voices, Joan traveled in May 1428 from Domrémy to Vaucouleurs, the nearest stronghold still loyal to the Dauphin, where she asked the captain of the garrison, Robert de Baudricourt, for permission to join the Dauphin. He did not take the 16-year-old girl and her visions seriously, and she returned home. Joan went to Vaucouleurs again in January 1429. This time her quiet firmness and piety gained her the respect of the people, and the captain, persuaded that she was neither a witch nor feebleminded, allowed her to go to the Dauphin at Chinon.

She left Vaucouleurs about February 13, dressed in men's clothes and accompanied by six men-at-arms. Crossing territory held by the enemy, and traveling for 11 days, she reached Chinon.

Joan went at once to the castle occupied by the Dauphin Charles. He was uncertain whether to receive her, but two days later he granted her an audience. Charles had hidden himself among his courtiers, but Joan made straight for him and told him that she wished to go to battle against the English and that she would have him crowned at Reims. On the Dauphin's orders, she was immediately interrogated by ecclesiastical authorities in the presence of Jean, duc d'Alençon, a relative of Charles, who showed himself well-disposed toward her. For three weeks, she was further questioned at Poitiers by eminent theologians who were allied to the Dauphin's cause. These examinations, the record of which has not survived, were occasioned by the ever-present fear of heresy following the end of the Great Schism in 1417. Joan told the ecclesiastics that it was not at Poitiers but at Orléans that she would give proof of her mission; forthwith, on March 22, she dictated letters of defiance to the English. In their report the churchmen suggested that in view of the desperate situation of Orléans, which had been under English siege for months, the Dauphin would be well-advised to make use of her.

Joan returned to Chinon. At Tours, during April, the Dauphin provided her with a military household of several men; Jean d'Aulon became her squire, and she was joined by her brothers Jean and Pierre. She had her standard painted with an image of Christ in Judgment and a banner made bearing the name of Jesus. When the question of a sword was brought up, she declared that it would be found in the church of Sainte-Catherine-de-Fierbois, and one was in fact discovered there.

Action at Orléans

Troops numbering several hundred men were mustered at Blois, and on April 27 they set out for Orléans. The city, besieged since October 12, 1428, was almost totally surrounded by a ring of English strongholds. When Joan and one of the French commanders, La Hire, entered with supplies on April 29, she was told that action must be deferred until further reinforcements could be brought in.

On the evening of May 4, when Joan was resting, she suddenly sprang up, apparently inspired, and announced that she must go and attack the English. Having herself armed, she hurried out to the east of the city toward an English fort where, indeed, an engagement of which she had not been told was taking place. Her arrival roused the French, and they took the fort. The next day Joan addressed another of her letters of defiance to the English. On the morning of May 6, she crossed to the south bank of the river and advanced toward another fort. The English immediately evacuated it in order to defend a stronger position nearby, but Joan and La Hire attacked them there and took it by storm. Very early on May 7 the French advanced against the fort of Les Tourelles. Joan was wounded but quickly returned to the fight; it was thanks in part to her example that the French commanders maintained the attack until the English capitulated. Next day the English were seen to be retreating, but, because it was a Sunday, Joan refused to allow any pursuit.

Victories and Coronation

Joan left Orléans on May 9 and met Charles at Tours. She urged him to make haste to Reims to be crowned. Though he hesitated because some of his more prudent counselors were advising him to undertake the conquest of Normandy, Joan's importunity ultimately carried the day. It was decided, however, first to clear the English out of the other towns along the Loire River. Joan met her friend the duc d'Alençon, who had been made lieutenant general of the French armies, and they moved off together, taking a town and an important bridge. They next attacked Beaugency, whereupon the English retreated into the castle. Then, notwithstanding the opposition of the Dauphin and Georges de La Trémoille, one of his favorites, and despite the reserve of Alençon, Joan received the Constable de Richemont, who was under suspicion at the French court. After making him swear fidelity, she accepted his help. Shortly thereafter the castle of Beaugency was surrendered.

The French and English armies came face to face at Patay on June 18, 1429. Joan promised success to the French, saying that Charles would win a greater victory that day than any he had won so far. The victory was indeed complete; the English army was routed and with it, finally, its reputation for invincibility.

Instead of pressing home their advantage by a bold attack upon Paris, Joan and the French commanders turned back to rejoin the Dauphin, who was staying with La Trémoille at Sully-sur-Loire. Again Joan urged upon Charles the need to go on swiftly to Reims. He vacillated, however; and as he meandered through the towns along the Loire, Joan accompanied him, arguing all the while in an attempt to vanquish his hesitancy and prevail over the counselors who advised delay. She was not unaware of the dangers and difficulties involved but declared them of no account. Finally, she won Charles to her view.

From Gien, where the army began to assemble, the Dauphin sent out the customary letters of summons to the coronation. Joan wrote two letters: one of exhortation to the people of Tournai, always loyal to Charles, the other a challenge to Philip the Good, duke of Burgundy. She and the Dauphin set out on the march to Reims on June 29. Before arriving at Troyes, Joan wrote to the inhabitants, promising them pardon if they would submit. They countered by sending a friar, the popular preacher Brother Richard to take stock of her. Though he returned full of enthusiasm for the Maid and her mission, the townsfolk decided after all to remain loyal to the Anglo-Burgundian regime. The Dauphin held a council, and Joan proposed that the town be attacked. The next morning she began the assault, and the citizens at once asked for terms.

The royal army then marched on to Châlons. Despite an earlier decision to resist, the Count-Bishop handed the keys of the town to Charles. On July 16, the royal army reached Reims, which opened its gates. The coronation took place on July 17, 1429. Joan was present at the consecration, standing with her banner not far from the altar. After the ceremony she knelt before Charles, calling him her king for the first time. That same day she wrote to the duke of Burgundy, adjuring him to make peace with the king and to withdraw his garrisons from the royal fortresses.

Ambitions for Paris

Charles VII left Reims on July 20, and for a month the army paraded through Champagne and the Île-de-France. On August 2, the king decided on a retreat from Provins to the Loire, a move that implied abandoning any plan to attack Paris. The loyal towns that would thus have been left to the enemy's mercy expressed some alarm. Joan, who was opposed to Charles's decision, wrote to reassure the citizens of Reims on August 5, saying that the duke of Burgundy, then in possession of Paris, had made a fortnight's truce, after which it was hoped that he would yield Paris to the king. In fact, on August 6, English troops prevented the royal army from crossing the Seine at Bray, much to the delight of Joan and the commanders, who hoped that Charles would attack Paris. Everywhere acclaimed, Joan was now, according to a 15th-century chronicler, the idol of the French. She herself felt that the purpose of her mission had been achieved.

Near Senlis, on August 14, the French and English armies again confronted each other. This time only skirmishes took place, neither side daring to start a battle, though Joan carried her standard up to the enemy's earthworks and openly challenged them. Meanwhile Compiègne, Beauvais, Senlis, and other towns north of Paris surrendered to the king. Soon afterward, on August 28, a four months' truce for all the territory north of the Seine was concluded with the Burgundians.

Joan, however, was becoming more and more impatient; she thought it essential to take Paris. She and Alençon were at Saint-Denis on the northern outskirts of Paris on August 26, and the Parisians began to organize their defenses. Charles arrived on September 7, and an attack was launched on September 8, directed between the gates of Saint-Honoré and Saint-Denis. The Parisians could be in no doubt of Joan's presence among the besiegers; she stood forward on the earthworks, calling on them to surrender their city to the king of France. Wounded, she continued to encourage the soldiers until she had to abandon the attack. Though the next day she and Alençon sought to renew the assault, they were ordered by Charles's council to retreat.

Further Struggle

Charles VII retired to the Loire, Joan following him. At Gien, which they reached on September 22, the army was disbanded. Alençon and the other captains went home; only Joan remained with the king. Later, when Alençon was planning a campaign in Normandy, he asked the king to let Joan rejoin him, but La Trémoille and other courtiers dissuaded him. Joan went with the king to Bourges. In October she was sent against Saint-Pierre-le-Moûtier; through her courageous assault, with only a few men, the town was taken. Joan's army then laid siege to La Charité-sur-Loire; short of munitions, they appealed to neighboring towns for help. The supplies arrived too late, and after a month they had to withdraw.

Joan then rejoined the king, who was spending the winter in towns along the Loire. Late in December 1429, Charles issued letters ennobling Joan, her parents, and her brothers. Early in 1430 the duke of Burgundy began to threaten Brie and Champagne. The inhabitants of Reims became alarmed, and Joan wrote in March to assure them of the king's concern and to promise that she would come to their defense. When the duke moved up to attack Compiègne, the townsfolk determined to resist, and in late March or early April Joan left the king and set out to their aid, accompanied only by her brother Pierre, her squire Jean d'Aulon, and a small troop of men-at-arms. She arrived at Melun in the middle of April, and it was no doubt her presence that prompted the citizens there to declare themselves for Charles VII.

Joan was at Compiègne by May 14, 1430. There she found Renaud de Chartres, archbishop of Reims, and Louis I de Bourbon, comte de Vendôme, a relative of the king. With them she went on to Soissons, where the townspeople refused them entry. Renaud and Vendôme therefore decided to return south of the Marne and Seine rivers; but Joan refused to accompany them, preferring to return to her "good friends" in Compiègne.

Capture, Trial, and Execution

On her way back Joan heard that John of Luxembourg, the captain of a Burgundian company, had laid siege to Compiègne. Hurrying on, she entered Compiègne under cover of darkness. The next afternoon, May 23, she led a sortie and twice repelled the Burgundians but was eventually outflanked by English reinforcements and compelled to retreat. Remaining until the last to protect the rear guard while they crossed the Oise River, she was unhorsed and could not remount. She gave herself up and, with her brother Pierre and Jean d'Aulon, was taken to Margny, where the duke of Burgundy came to see her. In telling the people of Reims of Joan's capture, Renaud de Chartres accused her of rejecting all counsel and acting willfully. Charles, who was working toward a truce with the duke of Burgundy, made no attempts to save her.

John of Luxembourg sent Joan and Jean d'Aulon to his castle in Vermandois. When she tried to escape in order to return to Compiègne, he sent her to one of his more distant castles. There, though she was treated kindly, she became more and more distressed at the predicament of Compiègne. Her desire to escape became so great that she jumped from the top of a tower, falling unconscious into the moat. She was not seriously hurt, and when she had recovered, she was taken to Arras, a town adhering to the duke of Burgundy.

News of her capture had reached Paris on May 25. The next day the theology faculty of the University of Paris, which had taken the English side, requested the duke of Burgundy to turn her over for judgment either to the chief inquisitor or to the bishop of Beauvais, Pierre Cauchon, in whose diocese she had been seized. The university wrote also, to the same effect, to John of Luxembourg; and on July 14 the Bishop of Beauvais presented himself before the duke of Burgundy asking, on his own behalf and in the name of the English king, that the Maid be handed over in return for a payment of 10,000 francs. The duke passed on the demand to John of Luxembourg, and by January 3, 1431, she was in the bishop's hands.

The trial was fixed to take place at Rouen. Joan was moved to a tower in the castle of Bouvreuil, which was occupied by the earl of Warwick, the English commander at Rouen. Though her offenses against the Lancastrian monarchy were common knowledge, Joan was brought to trial before a church court because the theologists at the University of Paris, as arbiter in matters concerning the faith, insisted that she be tried as a heretic. Her beliefs were not strictly orthodox, according to the criteria for orthodoxy laid down by many theologians of the period. She was no friend of the church militant on Earth (which perceived itself as in spiritual combat with the forces of evil), and she threatened its hierarchy through her claim that she communicated directly with God by means of visions or voices. Further, her trial might serve to discredit Charles VII by demonstrating that he owed his coronation to a witch, or at least a heretic. Her two judges were to be Cauchon, bishop of Beauvais, and Jean Lemaître, the vice-inquisitor of France.

The Trial

Beginning January 13, 1431, statements taken in Lorraine and elsewhere were read before the Bishop and his assessors; they were to provide the framework for Joan's interrogation. Summoned to appear before her judges on February 21, Joan asked for permission to attend mass beforehand, but it was refused on account of the gravity of the crimes with which she was charged, including attempted suicide in having jumped into the moat. She was ordered to swear to tell the truth and did so swear, but she always refused to reveal the things she had said to Charles. Cauchon forbade her to leave her prison, but Joan insisted that she was morally free to attempt escape. Guards were then assigned to remain always inside the cell with her, and she was chained to a wooden block and sometimes put in irons.

Between February 21 and March 24, she was interrogated nearly a dozen times. On every occasion, she was required to swear anew to tell the truth, but she always made it clear that she would not necessarily divulge everything to her judges since they were enemies of King Charles. The report of this preliminary questioning was read to her on March 24, and apart from two points she admitted its accuracy.

When the trial proper began a day or so later, it took two days for Joan to answer the 70 charges that had been drawn up against her. These were based mainly on the contention that her whole attitude and behavior showed blasphemous presumption: in particular, that she claimed for her pronouncements the authority of divine revelation; prophesied the future; endorsed her letters with the names of Jesus and Mary, thereby identifying herself with the novel and suspect cult of the Name of Jesus; professed to be assured of salvation; and wore men's clothing. Perhaps the most serious charge was of preferring what she believed to be the direct commands of God to those of the church.

On March 31, she was questioned again on several points about which she had been evasive, notably on the question of her submission to the church. In her position, obedience to the court that was trying her was inevitably made a test of such submission. She did her best to avoid this trap, saying she knew well that the church militant could not err, but it was to God and to her saints that she held herself answerable for her words and actions. The trial continued, and the 70 charges were reduced to 12, which were sent for consideration to many eminent theologians in both Rouen and Paris.

Meanwhile, Joan fell sick in prison and was attended by two doctors. She received a visit on April 18 from Cauchon and his assistants, who exhorted her to submit to the church. Joan, who was seriously ill and obviously thought she was dying, begged to be allowed to go to confession and receive Holy Communion and to be buried in consecrated ground. But they continued to badger her, receiving only her constant response "I am relying on our Lord, I hold to what I have already said." They became more insistent on May 9, threatening her with torture if she did not clarify certain points. She answered that even if they tortured her to death she would not reply differently, adding that in any case she would afterward maintain that any statement she might make had been extorted from her by force. In face of this commonsense fortitude her interrogators, by a majority of 10 to three, decided on May 12 that torture would be useless.

Joan was informed on May 23 of the decision of the University of Paris that if she persisted in her errors she would be turned over to the secular authorities. Only they, and not the church, could carry out the death sentence of a condemned heretic.

Abjuration, Relapse, and Execution

Apparently nothing further could be done. Joan was taken out of prison for the first time in four months on May 24 and conducted to the cemetery of the church of Saint-Ouen, where her sentence was to be read out. First she was made to listen to a sermon by one of the theologians in which he violently attacked Charles VII, provoking Joan to interrupt him because she thought he had no right to attack the king, a "good Christian," and should confine his strictures to her. After the sermon was ended, she asked that all the evidence on her words and deeds be sent to Rome. But her judges ignored her appeal to the Pope, to whom, under God, she would be answerable, and began to read out the sentence abandoning her to the secular power. Hearing this dreadful pronouncement, Joan quailed and declared she would do all that the church required of her. She was presented with a form of abjuration, which must already have been prepared. She hesitated in signing it, eventually doing so on condition that it was "pleasing to our Lord." She was then condemned to perpetual imprisonment or, as some maintain, to incarceration in a place habitually used as a prison. In any case, the judges required her to return to her former prison.

The vice-inquisitor had ordered Joan to put on women's clothes, and she obeyed. But two or three days later, when the judges and others visited her and found her again in male attire, she said she had made the change of her own free will, preferring men's clothes. They then pressed other questions, to which she answered that the voices of

Saint Catherine and Saint Margaret had censured her "treason" in making an abjuration. These admissions were taken to signify relapse, and on May 29 the judges and 39 assessors agreed unanimously that she must be handed over to the secular officials.

The next morning, Joan received permission, unprecedented for a relapsed heretic, to make her confession and receive Communion. Accompanied by two Dominicans, she was then led to the Place du Vieux-Marché. There she endured one more sermon, and the sentence abandoning her to the secular arm—that is, to the English and their French collaborators—was read out in the presence of her judges and a great crowd. The executioner seized her, led her to the stake, and lit the pyre. A Dominican consoled Joan, who asked him to hold high a crucifix for her to see and to shout out the assurances of salvation so loudly that she should hear him above the roar of the flames. To the last she maintained that her voices were sent of God and had not deceived her. According to the rehabilitation proceedings of 1456, few witnesses of her death seem to have doubted her salvation, and they agreed that she died a faithful Christian. A few days later, the English king and the University of Paris formally published the news of Joan's execution.

Almost 20 years afterward, on his entry into Rouen in 1450, Charles VII ordered an inquiry into the trial. Two years later the cardinal legate Guillaume d'Estouteville made a much more thorough investigation. Finally, on the order of Pope Calixtus III following a petition from the d'Arc family, proceedings were instituted in 1455–56 that revoked and annulled the sentence of 1431. Joan was canonized by Pope Benedict XV on May 16, 1920.

ISABELLA I

(b. April 22, 1451, Madrigal de las Altas Torres, Castile—d. Nov. 26, 1504, Medina del Campo, Spain)

Together with her husband, Ferdinand II of Aragon (Ferdinand V of Castile), Queen Isabella I ruled Castile (1474–1504) and Aragon (1479–1504). Their rule effected the permanent union of Spain and the beginning of an overseas empire in the "New World," led by Christopher Columbus under Isabella's sponsorship.

Early Life

Isabella was the daughter of John II of Castile and his second wife, Isabella of Portugal. Three years after her birth, her half brother became king as Henry IV. Despite the fact that she had a younger brother, Alfonso, and that her early years were spent quietly with her mother at Arévalo, Isabella was soon drawn into Castilian politics. She was brought to court when she was 13 in order to be under the king's eye. At first the opposition to Henry IV gathered around Alfonso, but when the latter died in July 1468, the rebellious magnates naturally turned to Isabella. She did not, however, play the role thus designed for her, and the fruit of her wisdom was recognition as his heiress by Henry IV at the agreement known as the Accord of Toros de Guisando (September 19, 1468).

As heiress of Castile, Isabella and her future marriage became a matter of increasing diplomatic activity at home and abroad. Portugal, Aragon, and France each put forward a marriage candidate. Henry seems to have wanted his half sister to marry Afonso V, king of Portugal. Between the Portuguese and Aragonese candidates, she herself, no doubt assisted in her decision by her small group of councillors, came down in favor of Ferdinand of Aragon. A third suitor, the French duc de Guiènne, was sidestepped, and without Henry's approval she married Ferdinand in October 1469 in the palace of Juan de Vivero, at Valladolid. The prospect of an Aragonese consort led to the development of an anti-Aragonese party that put forward the claims of a rival heiress, Henry's daughter Joan, known as la Beltraneja by those who believed that her true father was Beltrán de la Cueva, duque de Albuquerque. The king encouraged this group by going back on the accord of 1468 on the grounds that Isabella had shown disobedience to the crown in marrying Ferdinand without the royal consent. He now rejected Isabella's claim to the throne and preferred that of Joan, for whom he sought the hand of the duc de Guiènne. Although Isabella and Henry were to some extent reconciled, the long-threatened war of succession broke out at once when the king died in 1474.

Reign

When Henry died, Isabella was in Segovia, which was secured for her claim. She was supported by an important group of Castilian nobles, including Cardinal Pedro González de Mendoza, the constable of Castile (a Velasco), and the admiral (an Enríquez), who was related to Ferdinand's mother. The opposing faction, which put forward the counterclaims of Joan, included the archbishop of Toledo; a former supporter, the master of Calatrava (an influential military order); and the powerful young Marqués de Villena. They were supported by Afonso V of Portugal, who hastened to invade Castile and there betrothed himself to Joan. The first four years of Isabella's reign were thus occupied by a civil war, which ended in defeat for her Castilian opponents and for the Portuguese king (February 24, 1479). Upon the death of John II of Aragon in the same year, the kingdoms of Castile and

Aragon came together in the persons of their rulers.

Spain emerged as a united country, but it was long before this personal union would lead to effective political unification. Indeed, in his first will (1475), Ferdinand made Isabella his heir in Aragon and openly declared the advantages his subjects would derive from the union with Castile. But each kingdom continued to be governed according to its own institutions.

The two sovereigns were certainly united in aiming to end the long process of Reconquista by taking over the kingdom of Granada—the last Muslim stronghold in Spain. In the end, however, the conquest (which began in 1482) proved difficult and drawn out, and it strained the finances of Castile. Although some of the features of the campaign were medieval (such as the order of battle), others were novel. Isabella took a close interest in the conduct of the war and seems to have been responsible for improved methods of supply and for the establishment of a military hospital. In 1491, she and Ferdinand set up a forward headquarters at Santa Fe, close to their ultimate objective, and there they stayed until Granada fell on January 2, 1492.

While she was at Santa Fe, another event with which the queen was to become personally associated was in the making. Columbus visited her there to enlist support for the voyage that was to result in the European settlement of America. Although the story of her offering to pledge her jewels to help finance the expedition cannot be accepted, and Columbus secured only limited financial support from her, Isabella and her councillors must receive credit for making the decision to approve the momentous voyage. The terms on which the expedition was to set out to discover a new route to the Indies were drawn up on April 17, 1492. The New World that was explored as a result of that decision was, with papal confirmation, annexed to the crown of Castile, in accordance with existing practice in regard to such previous Atlantic discoveries as the Canary Islands.

The queen and her advisers hardly needed Columbus to remind them of the opportunity now offered for the spreading of Christianity. Yet the unexpected discoveries quickly brought fresh problems to Isabella, not the least of which was the relationship between the newly discovered "Indians" and the crown of Castile. The queen and her councillors were more ready to recognize the rights of the Indians than was Columbus; she ordered some of those he had brought back as slaves to be released. The queen was still concerned with these problems when she died in 1504.

Meanwhile, in 1480, the Inquisition had been set up in Andalusia. There is little doubt that this represented the culmination of a long and popular movement against non-Christians and doubtful converts, which had manifested itself frequently in the late Middle Ages in Castile. The expulsion in 1492 of those Jews who refused conversion was the logical result of the establishment of the Inquisition. Yet, however meritorious the expulsion may have seemed at the time in order to achieve greater religious and political unity, judged by its economic consequences alone, the loss of this valuable element in Spanish society was a serious mistake.

Hallmarks of Her Reign

It is difficult to disentangle Isabella's personal responsibility for the achievements of her reign from those of Ferdinand. But, undoubtedly, she played a large part in establishing the court as a center of influence. With her blue eyes, her fair or chestnut hair, and her jewels and magnificent dresses, she must have made a striking figure. At the same time, display was matched with religious feeling.

Her choice of spiritual advisers brought to the fore such different and remarkable men as Hernando de Talavera and Cardinal Cisneros. A policy of reforming the Spanish churches had begun early in the 15th century, but the movement gathered momentum only under Isabella and Talavera.

When, in 1492, Talavera became archbishop of Granada, his place at the queen's side was taken by Cisneros, for whom the monarchs secured the crucial position of archbishop of Toledo in 1495. The monarchs were interested in the reform of the secular clergy and still more in the orders of monks, friars, and nuns; Isabella took a particular interest in the reform of the Poor Clares, an order of Franciscan nuns. Although when she died there was still much to be done, the rulers and Cisneros together had gone far toward achieving their goals.

Although Isabella (who was known by the epithet "the Catholic," Spanish: "la Católica") was intensely pious and orthodox in her beliefs, she could be both imperious and pertinacious in her dealings with the papacy. This was particularly true when she thought the pope was making bad appointments to Spanish benefices or in any way encroaching on the customary rights of the crown over the Spanish churches. For example, for the vacant see of Cuenca in 1478 she rejected the Italian cardinal appointed by the pope, who four years later accepted her alternative Spanish candidate. Subsequently, she successfully rejected the suggestion that the pope's nephew should become archbishop of Sevilla. In seeking to control appointments to Castilian sees, Isabella was not simply inspired by national sentiments. She also sought candidates of high standards; judged by her choices of men such as Talavera and Cisneros, Isabella was remarkably effective in achieving her objective.

Isabella was almost as interested in education as she was in religion. After she reached the age of 30, she acquired proficiency in Latin. At court she encouraged such notable scholars as Pietro Martire d'Anghiera, whom she set up as the head of a new palace school for the sons of the nobility. Naturally, many of the outstanding literary works of her reign, such as Antonio de Nebrija's *Gramática Castellana* (1492; Castilian grammar), were dedicated to her. She was also the patron of Spanish and Flemish artists, and part of her extensive collection of pictures survives.

Later Years

The last decade of her reign took place against a background of family sorrows brought about by the deaths of her only son and heir, Juan (1497); of her daughter Isabella, queen of Portugal, in childbirth (1498); and of her grandchild Miguel (1500), who might have brought about a personal union between Spain and Portugal. Instead, her daughter Joan, wife of Philip I and mother of the Holy Roman emperor Charles V, became the heiress of Castile. However, this offered little comfort to the queen because by 1501 Joan had already shown signs of the mental imbalance that would later earn her the title of "the Mad."

One of the achievements of Isabella's last decade was undoubtedly the success with which she and Ferdinand, acting on her initiative, extended their authority over the military orders of Alcántara, Calatrava, and Santiago, thus giving the crown control over their vast property and patronage. These orders had been exploited for too long by the nobility and were the subject of intense rivalry among those who sought to be elected master of one or other of them. In 1487, Ferdinand became grand master of Calatrava, and by 1499 he had acquired the grand masterships of Alcántara and Santiago. With the capture of Granada, the main work of the orders had been done, and a process that envisaged their ultimate absorption into the lands of the crown was logical and sensible. Throughout her long reign, Isabella also strove to strengthen royal authority at the expense of the Cortes (Spanish parliament) and the towns.

Good sense and statesmanship were equally reflected in Isabella's will and codicil. Because she left no memoirs, her will is in many ways the most reliable picture of her. In it she sums up her aspirations and her awareness of how much she and Ferdinand had been unable to do. With prudence she comments on the basis of her political program—the unity of the states of the Iberian Peninsula, the maintenance of control over the Strait of Gibraltar, and a policy of expansion into Muslim North Africa, of just rule for the Indians of the New World, and of reform in the church at home. If the overall impression is inevitably piecemeal, it is also clear that Isabella gave to her successors an exceptional document. It assures scholars that in allotting to Isabella the foremost place among their rulers, Spaniards do not misjudge this remarkable woman.

Glossary

abjuration: The act of renouncing or giving up, frequently under oath.

apostolic age: Early period in the Christian church dominated by the actions of those personally known to Jesus or his disciples.

concubine: A woman who lives with a man as his wife, without actually being married to him.

consort: A companion or partner; the spouse of royalty.

extant: Still in existence.

funerary: Suitable for or associated with burial.

hypostyle hall: A building with a roof or ceiling supported by rows of columns.

obelisk: A tall, tapered, four-sided shaft of stone, usually with a pointed pyramidal top.

pernicious: Causing great harm or death.

regnal: Calculated from the beginning of a monarch's reign.

sarcophagus: A highly decorated coffin that typically is not buried.

stelae: Stone slab used as a grave marker or a memorial device.

thiasos: Greek term for a community of women.

titulary: The royal protocol adopted by Egyptian sovereigns.

unguent: A healing ointment.

veneration: To show profound respect.

For More Information

BOOKS

Albee, Sarah. *Troublemakers in Trousers: Women and What They Wore to Get Things Done.* Watertown, MA: Charlesbridge, 2022.

McManus, Lori. *Ancient Civilizations: Women Who Made a Difference.* New York, NY: Children's Press, 2023.

Skelley, Billie Holladay. *Hypatia: Ancient Alexandria's Female Scholar.* Springfield, MO: Paperback Press, 2021.

Wilson, Seán Michael, Murasaki Shikibu, and Inko. *Tale of Genji: The Manga Edition.* Clarendon, VT: Tuttle Publishing, 2022.

WEBSITES

History Cooperative: The Queens of Egypt
historycooperative.org/queens-of-egypt/
Learn more about Hatshepsut, Nefertiti, Cleopatra, and other queens of ancient Egypt in this article.

National Geographic Kids: Joan of Arc
kids.nationalgeographic.com/history/article/joan-of-arc
This article provides some background information on Joan of Arc, accompanied by paintings depicting scenes from her life.

Poems of Sappho
www.uh.edu/~cldue/texts/sappho.html
An English translation of Sappho's ancient Greek poetry is presented on this page.

Poetry in Translation: Christine de Pisan
www.poetryintranslation.com/PITBR/French/ChristineDePisanRondeaux.php
You can read English translations of some of Christine de Pisan's medieval poetry on this page.

Index